Yeppa Part III

We

1. Yepp the Yeppa

Lyrics for the kick

click

And the question is there

which means Yeppa?

This is as clear as

without going into a search
engine

it can be seen

Yepp say to Yeppa

the means to affirm

2. Amazing like

Amazing is the word

The sounds good all the time

but in English only

Amazing is the pure

Be pleasantly surprised

with a rhyme

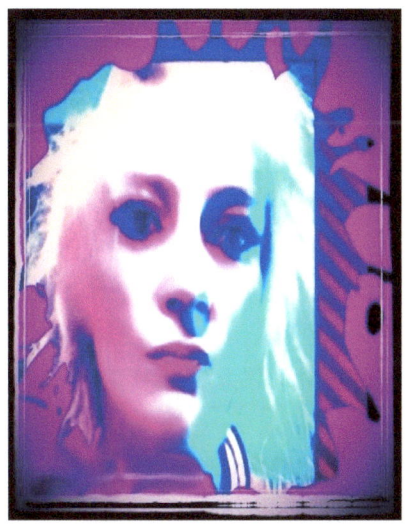

3.   The   Hingugger   hits   the eyecatcher

Images are an eye-catching

its ranking

Colloquially Hingugger

Sweet as Sugar

Eyecatcher at the center

everything revolves around

The view from sticking

in an effort

see the Beautiful

to understand

4. It's raining cats and dogs

It's raining cats and dogs

in strong bursts

"It rains cats and dogs"

it is nevertheless

it's raining cats and dogs

is in the English-speaking world
everyone is talking about

this is very normal

speak and formally

5. The Cat and the award

The cat is a sweet animal
strives forward with curiosity
playful, cuddly and individually
slowly but quickly
1873 arose the saying
"Couriosity killed the cat" -
Too many experiments are a curse

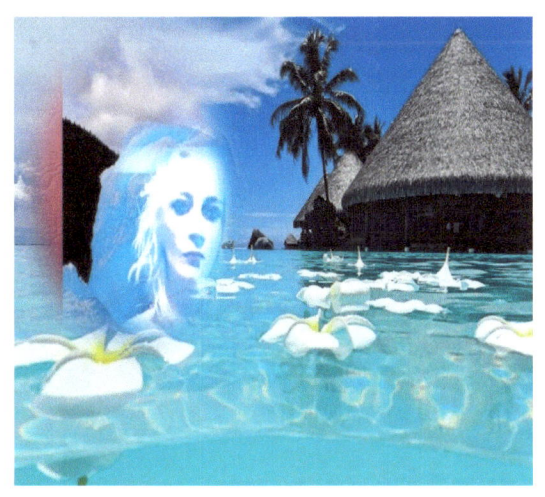

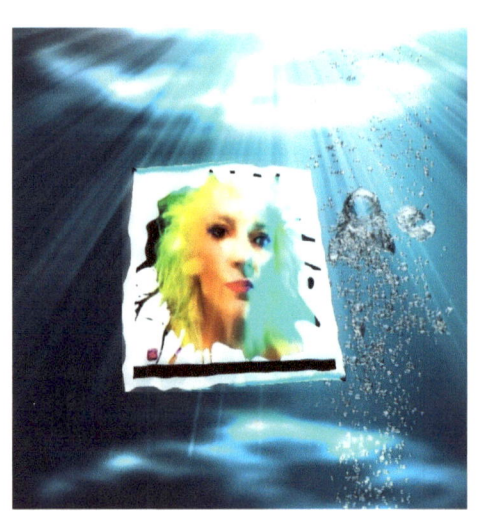

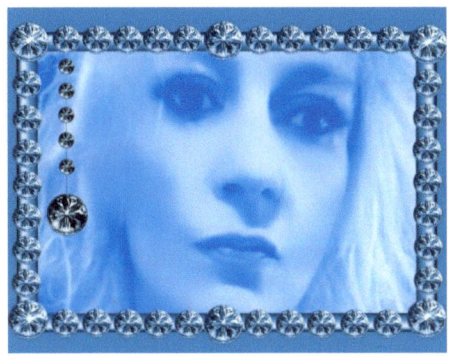

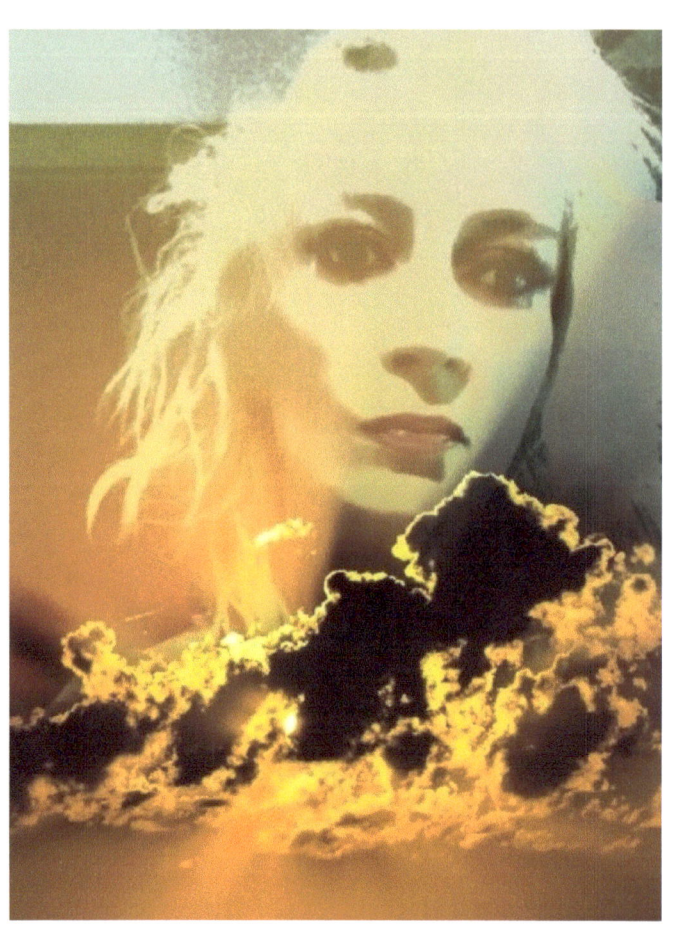

6. Making of

From a novel is a trilogy

from the poetry

is a multi-part band

Languages from around the country

only in German language

then translates the matter

naturally into English is compulsory

some works also in the Arab

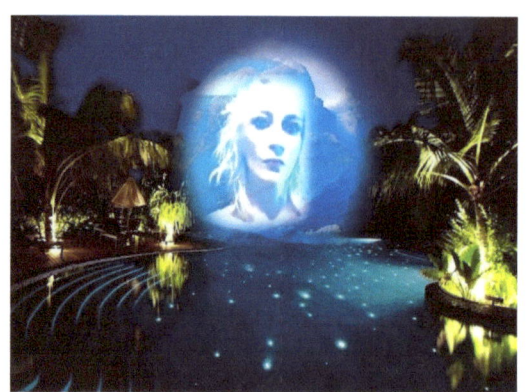

7. Languages and profiles

Our Author Profiles

have many

Languages

in at least seven different they
are published

to assist in the understanding

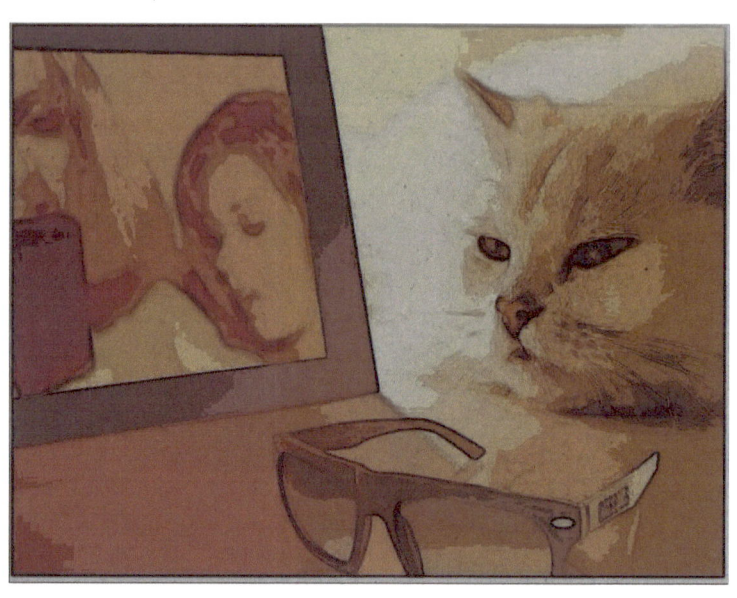

8. Yeppa?

Yepp it is

Yeppa na klar

the languages

the red thread

runs through Yeppa

and does not lose

To obtain information

and develop artistic

9. From School

Latin Lives by sentence
structure and Gerund

Is a refuge

the grammar

It is interesting, for example,

gender page

The tree is female

view from Latin

Arbor - Arboris

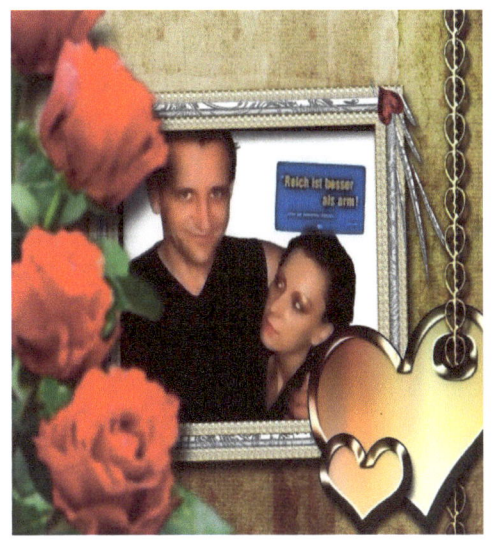

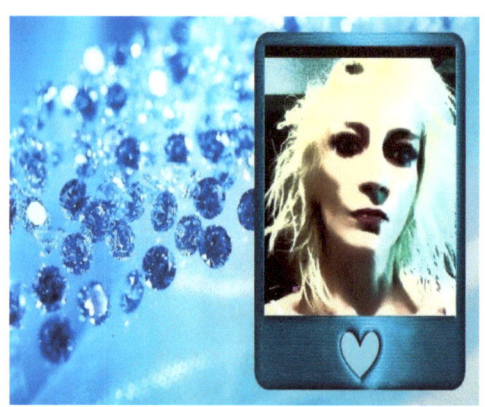

10. Around the corner

The globe is global
this is normal
Enrichment in sight
this is the light

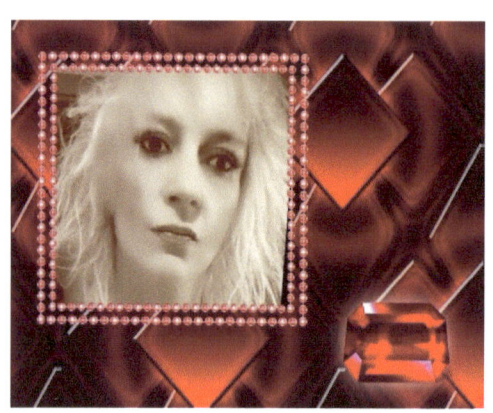

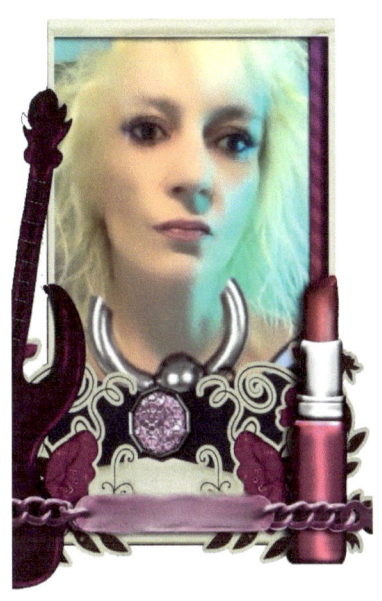

We say Yeppa

www.ingramcontent.com/pod-product-compliance
Lightning Source LLC
Chambersburg PA
CBHW041618180526
45159CB00002BC/911